Antibodies

Alexandra Sashe

Antibodies

Shearsman Books

First published in the United Kingdom in 2013 by
Shearsman Books
50 Westons Hill Drive
Emersons Green
BRISTOL
BS16 7DF

Shearsman Books Ltd Registered Office
30–31 St. James Place, Mangotsfield, Bristol BS16 9JB
(this address not for correspondence)

www.shearsman.com

ISBN 978-1-84861-283-9

ACKNOWLEDGEMENTS
Some of these have previously appeared in the following journals:
The Black Herald, Dear Sir, Decanto, The Delinquent, Fire, Frogmore Papers,
Inclement, The Journal, Loch Raven Review, La Reata, Paroles des Jours,
Poetry Salzburg Review, Shearsman, Upstairs at Duroc.

Contents

Part II

"You may safely offer me snow."

—Paul Celan
from *Breathcrystal*

Part I

Autumnal

he said it had been oleander shadows
the vertical arm-raised
shadows,
proofless as our arms—
                    as motherless.

a frail bark that contains
voice,
the st. christophers of the boulevard.

your tide, the nine p.m. winter contingencies.
my backwash, a déjà-vu fever.
so we wade, overloaded children.
so we lose, hands down.

She aims at hesitance with a sharp eye.
Someone shall respond—at the edge of the pond, she is
fishing the mirror creatures, to bring them
back to the initial stage
of evolution,

to swap skins with them,
her scrawny forearms for fins,
her fever for gills, her language for
the slime of algae, her eyes
for eyes on temples,
her sex for two, or
none.

There had been
a tree
(I remember)
years ago.
Not a garden. An empty space
centred around the trunk—
which gave a tree.

Perhaps that gave other
things
which I now don't remember.
I remember this much.
I might have remembered nothing.

But here is the tree:
a nameless solitary object
possibly of the family
of aspens, or maples, or other—
—or none
(for namelessness is what prevails).

It peeled every spring. No one
thought it unnatural.
No one thought anything—
and passed by,
or leaned back against it. (But I
saw no one leaning, ever).

So I remember the tree:
weals of roots
under the layer of asphalt,
      vacuum
pivoted on the branches.

Now people have grown older :
     and start leaning
     against the trunk.
(Though only occasionally, and for a short respite).
I should like
to wait for a couple of centuries
to see them loaded with years, to see them limp,
the hunchbacks, and wobble by, seeking relief
in the arboreal girth and uprightness,
their eyes closed, hollow…

(I will recall them, centuries later,
the human phantoms peeling off from the daylight.
No one shall see them. The asphalt cracks
with the roots of the dead tree.—

       So I
   will remember the dead tree.
      (which is what
   will have prevailed by then).

Shall I say silence is exhausted and my
hands now leave scratches on its grey bottom, and other

hands too had drawn
all over it the countless ideograms
which were to be their testimony—and are
their imploded cries.

It is north here, past midnight and windy;
and silence is an eroding soil.

And shall I say you are now
too exposed—
reclining on its slopes.

Heaven bound children, childless,
sodden with rain, wing-folded,
desert benches along the boulevards
walk
      blind,
when the bell gravitates the hour.
The heartsore beat and the air are theirs – they
measure each other.
A thousand paper birds
left
      to tear in their wake.

St. Anselm's Art

A counter-hand may yet recreate
our thresholds:
the ink-blue sky, a painless edge of an armchair.

I touch the cloths of your wounds—
you touch the ones of mine.   (Our pages and canvases
eclipse one another's prayers).

From our netherworld secrets you've learnt
to practice your St. Anselm's art.—I've learnt
how to stab myself deeper without dying.

We lie and dream
across the amplitude
of frozen
Venetian time.

Our eyes closed we slough
and blend
our distances
          with the nebbia.

unmoving as vision of snow
falling through the half-conscious
skin retains the dreamt
the thought
the known the barely
worded.

Indifference answers questions

whence the sounds rain down
on eaves and linens,

pre-beginnings and after-endings
heal
the rent in the circle.

Only one night's immobility: cells of hours
replace cells of space:

whence a courtyard—
silent and bare

like a footfall
receding.

It is time to start being towards winter,
to start being its advent
at 5 a.m. along the cornices, to share in its
milky shade of opacity. To start being windless and nettle.

from 5 a.m. to walk neatly into your pro-mnesis,
via the *Dorotheengaße*—with your swept house and face
that changes the angle,

and you
true, safe,
unlovable.

It is time to start being
towards winter.   To sift apart marbles
and broken marbles,
their dry sounds' prefiguration of a dawnless pilgrimage
into the rooms.   The season of ribs and invisible crows.

at 5 p.m. to brew a subtime
of the late oils and brown bitter
apophthegmatic roots of an ash tree.   Time to
cloth over the spoken
from the behind-faces.
To leave the knots undo their knots.

It is left to learn ochre
and vegetation,

an entry by the bound end of eternity.
To merit the noble
varnish and silence of

furniture, white unbreakable
porcelain,

to be kept among them
for the sake
of the rectitude

of their angles, to learn
from all that speaks of the not
otherwise.

Frost

What do we grow from an unused
day's hour? Where do we pour its ice,
its orphaned minutes?—
they hide their pupils behind the lowering eyelids:

we stay and listen out for an encounter—
and recognize it in glass
splinter against the floor tiles.

Where do we live, after—
having escaped from the day's non-hour,
ourselves unbroken,
the chill of our bare soles left on the floor tiles?—

    (or else, if we walked through its walls in and out,
        how could it endure, this silent tower,—and then if we walked
only in
        or out,
       and bore no harm at all?)

where—once its odour of violets
comes to fill our veins' vacuum—are we to place
                         hunger
outside veins, lungs, outside our
somnambulic insulation?—and how
             are we to tell hunger
from thirst—that is bound to lay its claim
upon every deserted quarter?

And if, in sleep,
we come to absolve us from ourselves,
draw the curtains and be released,
our eyes shut,—
then what do we do
so as to see   —in it—
                                    our freedom, and
to come to terms with it—we, its nameless victims?

Or else,
if we wake up and survive the illusion of being
freed from the non-hour,—then
                                    how
do we confront a window on the following morning?

    (and if we enter the following morning, what
    will uphold us as whole pieces,
    will they take, the whole pieces, grafted on our
    foreign bodies?)

But still,
if we swallow time's anaesthesia
and see that the windowpane doesn't mist over,
nor shutter, nor shed its instinctive necessity,
and all maintains
its immaculate order : (our mirrors false, our faces scarless),
    what will be left of us, if one morning
    morning starts at a wrong hour,
    and finds us alone, awake,
                                    in front
of our breath cloud,—
                                    a still tepid trace of us becoming
                                    part of the hoar-frost?

Common dream

Common as long
as unshared

Greenwich time, choice of cloth,
a table, an armchair: yours
in the afternight, mine—
in an underhour.

A window from which you see
the pavement, and I—
pavement plus you:
your needle movements
in and out the laws
of inertia,
                perspective and gravity.

Even snow,
hardly in our latitudes, is
eyes-closed
falling upon my…
                …upon your sill,
while my hand is warming over a glass of cognac,
while you are sleeping, seeing
                our common dream.

Later, in Vienna

For the white stretches of copper and flakes
uninterrupted
by the audio needle (but be it there still,
still blunting templewards)

past eleven, your presence
thickens you at the tablestead—
your silence domes over—*Griensteidl's*
prayer for verdigris.

Static,
compacted within
the eucharistic eyerooms and says,

strongly beyond renovation (as that
angel
who thus ceases not to be)
I moor time in the mirrors' stead:
we scoop one another with small cups
and learn not to run back
into our shells.

your (oracle's) hand

remove everything: turn everything into a died-
out sound, a whiff,
an echo,—a still
humid stroke of our tissue
over a wooden surface that had
finally lost its varnish,
and now could breathe, now could be,
unlooked at,
shedding us as reflections, opaque as we are,—
be.

    Let there subsist,
        through the vernal (or our) negligence

a piece of lace—for a
lampshade;

a sense of awaiting, like that at Easter,
so that what's always been there—comes;

a certain significant ochre (or brown) object
steeped in our language—to speak
for our lives, from
within their sacred silence;

a constant presence in this
or that form (an aftertaste,

foretaste, a tinge of colour,
a waft
bred under the thawing snow,
a presentiment of
a faraway-and-unknown awakening)—of a
strong bitter abysmal cold
sugary cruel speaking
of poverty plenitude truth our
ever before and after
one-ness

       flavour of tea.

Name me,
and let there subsist some of these,
a thousand years from now,
around the table, among you and I,
on one of the Sundays, in early March,
at an hour nearing
5 p.m.

Sadness prevails.   no longer
an anguish
nor a corkscrew
mentioned rapidly into the marrow.

felt
clothing off the internal borders
between the dusk and the following
resurrectional morning.

for long
crows' sparse names
will remain unevoked.
                    Sadness
retains its humid
throughout the season; our lips endure,
hands sustain on the milk we are
to warm over and over.

Sadness prevails. The retraced itinerary
of the homebound
flotsam jetsam
sunwreck moonwreck. A neat flock
of the white crows ever
migrating northwards.
Rubies and emeralds of their hearts auctioned
for a leftover
gingerbread of tomorrow. Alternation of apodoses and eves:
a first part of the
sublimated summer.

Ice, privilege
of the surface of water: reflects the sky,

contains it in.

Sadness prevails. and prevails
on itself,
on its ever-weathering soil, its dry salt

humid days'
demi-seasonal semi-detached sleep,
our half-
common half-mutual
complementation.

Sadness loyal to its orbit
describes the lower hemisphere—
the fluid line of the wing of a crow, pendant
to its broken tenor.

The sky descends in the guise of twilight,
fog is our naked hearing
thirsted by its exposure.
A thousand crows migrating eastwards : by-pass us.

    Our ear absorbs the dry
    the peeling rust of their voices.

Inescapable poignancy of a chair
overturned on the counter—

outlines chalked in black
on air—its sudden

stark immobility
in no one's light.   Like a blinded ox,

or a childhood
that choked on the dark and bred

all colours of shame
and fear

Like cold sweat of the homebound—
at an hour

that cuts in between the closing
time and the fog,

like fog's increasing proclivity
to turn sour in the mouth, to cut in

out of focus
between the quays and the eyes—

like eyes'
recourse to the eyelids'

simultaneous darkness.
Like what is alive

and breeds
all colours and shades

of anguish.

When the morning hours leave you
the left finds its way at your table:
de-shaped, it frees time from coherency—lays it
among the woodcracks.

Mind, conscious of the symmetry
of the elbow bones—aching, fragmentary—
is your skin; skin
mist-crocheted, lips still bleeding bourbon.

Veins' knotted dimensions weighed down with voices,
voices, echoes of voices, echoes
                        of echoes,

'Listen, I've found a seashell, listen, listen,
        it unearths the ocean,'—hears
                        ear long deaf to anything
                        but its own inner madness.

But
voices are blind, sight-flayed,
and multiple skins come off as dead skin.—Silence
shall answer questions, whence nothing shall come, and
nothing
shall go whither.

Faces upturn and watch the wounds
opening up in heavens:

I sit and rock in my rocking chair, as gods would rock
loaded with prayers,—as one
would sip one's existence
upon the third glass of the night sediments.

I lip the silence, as gods would curse
another spin of eternity,—

I close my eyes but don't flicker and fall,
as they would do
                 when they are
                            stars.

Here,
town—
a human mirage; reverse
gravity of the shoulder blades,
veins' knotted dimensions
pent-up in marble,

weighed down
by voices, voices… echoes
of voices, echoes

of echoes. Where—mouth
starves itself into soliloquies.

hardly anyone
could think of a line sharper, a knife
more brittle. Where—voices
are buried among the heavenstones.

By quarter past century
domes
dream of bichrome millennia
dream implosion,
inversion… Here

'I've found a seashell, listen, listen…
it unearths the ocean'—

hears
an ear long deaf to anything
but its own inner madness.

Stripped to a cell, to its alpha-
betic unit, flesh gasps.—Here
feel the caryatids'

asphyxia.

Snow is crows
(isolation of
pitch-black voices)
drawn surreal
across the land-
scape.

One cannot drown in snow, by association.
Even when feet are leaden
and winged by the land-
slide.

Crows are stitches
sewn apart
          they are not
born from an egg shell—
instead
sooted out from dawn's
fearful coagulating hours.

Their voices
dislodge the vertebrae
between time and topography,
spill over the margins
of one's presence,
deduce one
snowblind, down,
for ever—
        from one's
                solitude.

Demagnetized hand
still points blankly to north.
A tram still skirts the Ring
at midnight. And the forehead lines
of the Cardinal Albergati keep watch
over the city where I

finish my second glass, one too little,
pocket the change—and by dawn,
will perhaps
still
be.

A limpid tear-
pivoted essence
wells on the edges of our cuts.

We respond to it with a bow,
with an involuntary jerk of a shoulder.—
we recognize one another:
                              the two
        winged homicidal solitudes:
our paintbrushes, sounds and furies,
our jack-knife afternoons.

A thousand years across the field—
a third wheel
of a long de-wheeled barrow.
Deathless and birthless we halt, help one another off
with the wings,—our cries
counterpoint
the impossible birds in the heaven.

We close one another's wounds,—fall down
        and sleep in the hay.
Unloved, in our dreams we are
almost unhated,—almost, almost
                              forgotten.

In the above-grave's shade

I lie in my hands, temple
buried in *sauges*   a *sauge*-word, long begotten,
is born and a pilgrim.
Wakefulness draws a narrow circle, systoles until the word
has crossed the twilight. I learn a hidden nudity from the *sauges*
and disappear shade by shade
from all eyes.

Begotten anew, I speak the abode
of the above-grave,
and, with my back to the sun,
sit on the porches of its
noble opaque acoustics.

poison: soundless, still,
lake-dark,
it offers cries and sudden clarifications.
    no one can harm it, it lies in a drawer
    and conjures dreams: a fishmouth,
    mute, fleshy:
    opening, closing, opening, closing, opening…

I am a centre,
externally unavoidable—
eyes meet at the crossings
stitched through my heap and neck.

tongues—speeches
hurled over my shoulder,
my cardiac valve—subject of the
(super)human seismology.
    fingerbones, lake sailors, are
    wardens of agitation.

my lips—increasingly cherry-red
(although I address nobody), and all
the lapels and button holes
parataxize my nudity.

if only bones were my feathers, they
would have known how to be.
        but no,
        even bones are not feathers:
        they gallop nowhere, like trees in the wind.

(from the cycle 'Invocations')

Come here,
vicinity's miles distance,—lay your lines,
foreshortened, one over another.   I've been
Brunelleschi recently, and travelled north, and
now I know words and syncopal silences.
    So come, lay your forehead upon my centre,
    hide your fingerbones, drink from
    your -lessness,

break my fingerbones, blossoming vowels. Recall
the sunspot on the brown upholstery (and all
the generations I should
have stowed away in my bosom).   So come,
it's quarter past thirty. I'll give you
nothing,—
    come get your share.

come
as a voice ventri-
loquated through the aestival
air of
isolation. Through mid-June,
its foliage-eclipsed faces and
     non-faces: their encounters and
     non-encounters:

a monochrome time, its ceaseless
closing upon itself,
     its eventual immobility.

here, I hold up
the out- and in-laid threads—and others
who came
are bits of void ground between my fingers,

I—am
double-spaced, a margin
readied for a foot-note,
a palm-note, an eye-note, a tongue-note…
     what comes—
     comes as a voice's breath: a breather
     between my spirals and soliloquies.

I have intended
     you for this much.

So much wax for so many needles.

come over here to break the glassware, the windows, the
        moon's cup, to tear
the linens, the lacework, the pages
from mid-shelves, to burn
the candles, the bridges, the
stained clothes, the long long hours,
to drink up the dusk, the ice from
glasses, the sounds from fields, words
from my mouth, indifference
from my throat.

come, put your hand on the moist, warmest part
of my mind,
slip your fingers between the hidden,
dream-like curves of my being. Lift it up, open a little   what
you know as unconscious,   what I know as a
bound side.

Part II

Litany I

All dreams' depths are paved with drowned sailors.
an amalgam :
slow   eye-concave   sickly   defleshing
veined with emerald green.——weaned from hunger for oxygen
they unbelong apart   stir   ebb   envenom
the littoral spheres
of sleep.

all dreams' depths are paved with drowned sailors.
an amalgam: slow   eye-concave
sickly   defleshing   veined with emerald green.——weaned
from hunger for oxygen
they unbelong apart
stir   ebb   envenom
the littoral spheres
of sleep.

all dreams' depths are paved
with drowned sailors.
an amalgam : slow   eye-concave   sickly
defleshing   veined with emerald green.—
weaned from hunger for oxygen   they unbelong apart
stir   ebb   envenom
the littoral spheres

all   dreams' depths   are
paved
with   drowned   sailors

My riverman, our green comes
from the bottommost corners, we are
vitally sombre and ever-safe
with our barrels and arms
unloaded, inoculated against rust,
midnight navigation, syllables borne upon
the upper layers of water, all counter-spells and mast-
bound mariners,
their sharp edges and corrugated shells
of their astray-gone years.

Another degree of completion:

the necessity found in water
sublimation
of water in these
white Dionysian hands' encounter

(a wine-turned-water
mise-en-scène
of their casual separation)

yours
smooth out the sound-bred folds
mine
paste them into the words' ovary.

wherein
am re-born :
a unicorn's daughter—

sublimation
of non-encounters.

eyelash mechanism set to work
spin out its cruelty   grind to powder
petals and vanes,
moths, helicopters, words of belated farewell.

between the eyelashes   weather contingencies
ground to dust, stirred, sprinkled with salt, pepper,
burnt to ochre.

again and again they come to betray you,
close their humid deal with the wind and depart
in all four unbound directions,—and
lie in bed with the north and south.

The most butterflied spirits
home in the cloister, unhindered by walls
and earth and faces with eyes
they pass through—half-transform them into confessions,
count them for so many panes that have received the imprints
of their baptismal wings. And vaults of the eye sockets.
Skullfuls of self-conscious symmetry.

Their flight collects pollen and dust, ashes,
sounds of violins, cobwebs and silver. They fly
about the infinite,
unmistakably homeward.

Here I am am I am I not
betraying onwards the thresholds
the notes falling away and scatter
   in marbles over the floor
   tiles   and the sun gone

into the clouds' silent off-white redemption
   and am I am I not here
   recollected from marbles
   on the off-green of the mid-countries
   a railway wind breathing under
                           my fingers

All one could think of.

The smell of mazut and tobacco on empty stomach.
The ticket expires no sooner
than paper disintegrates.
Fog skins off your wake and leaves you alone
on the platform (alone: i.e. flesh and bones
with nothing
to hold them together except
for the memories and forebodings—i.e.
the selfsame deserting fog).

Poles comb through the hours... Wet nameless stations
glide over your retina
peeling the layers
of days and years...
A seat in the corner facing the opposite
zooming-away direction.

Coffee doesn't wash down
the smell of mazut and forebodings,
the taste of smoke in your mouth, nor
the aftertaste of withdrawal
from the other directions (those
the trains were taking this morning).

Coffee equals pain (its texture and its opacity;
mostly its composition: essence plus water). Perhaps

this is all one can think of:
the percentage of water in fog,
in years, in memory, in one's retina
stripped of its overcoating…

P.S. the other directions are soluble bodies
    in time, in fog, in forebodings…

P.P.S. the stains on the pane are part of the landscape
    seen from the train
    going…

★

(at a small cemetery
outside Vienna)

Stone: a homecoming
of a breath
down the desublimation path.

a stone-breath, roomful,
immortalized deeper
into the stone-oval.

We walk among, inscribe our words
that were
not words yet, not yet non-words,
not silence yet,—an insurmountable
articulation.

it wells over, lips our muteness
into tiny incisions.

We
can live there   in the ovals,
speak into one another across
our breath paths.

What we braid of the sunlight
is our danger—
a porcelain collection of equinoxes
sifted
from hand to hand,

conjuring up a larger space
in our breast pockets,

each thins out into a stalk of hay, or
de-sublimates into crystal,

spells us   and lies still…

It listens to our hearts welding
their choice into seconds.

: intervals :

down lined,
stone laid,
white pure furnaces

we cradle their tunes, nurse our muted
pulmonary exchanges,
write them into the hollows between
our ribs :

a quiet confidence in
                              time—
it will perfect our hearts
into supernovas

"The Garden of Eden"

nothing other than arm
        as bare as mine—nothing varied,
        as unalterable.

        one sound that set us apart—
        on one side—from other sounds.

        there lavender spreads out its annulets.
        we enter the right to abolish
        the volute motions of time:

an arm as bare as ours
        spheres around.
        what collects within the curve
        we knead with flour, seed and oil

        the bare of our arms
        doughs forth the light.

Volksgarten

you divine the place through bones' revelation. They have
their voice, they start to learn it. No obstructions
between bones and air, a lilac wind–   reencounter
of the bones and the green in the Volksgarten.

At the terminal one-hand crossroad, *Helmutplatz*,

the trees and the insignia
will stand the wind—you see it away, illegitimate here,
fragmented to its erroneous
southern gusts.   Hardly ever enough behind the pane,
I pray there be not what bears not
a boreal insignia, I pray it heal
the endamaged north in my eyes. (And it be island and
ramparts
and drawn-in bridges, and I be
foretaken here, and there forgiven foregone).

Behind the pane, ever more
no one and staircases—
their white inkspace. The *Helmutplatz* trees
are magicians of the deciduous:

they acquiesce to my one leaf,
and shed snow.

Do we share a rain and a bird

pilgrimage into her naked country,—

hour stretched over our

naked humid

leafless knowledge. Interlocuting and

equidistant

rainsoaked throbbing

inhabitants of

this northern part

of the Diameter.

Hourbone

    disjunction beyond the dusk

eye   conjures   a   concurrence of windows.

                               Mute

we carry along our homes

in   us.

          Rue des Ecoles :

you

  a juggler of gravity centres.

frost   will   perfect   us.

the streetlights
will consummate the mid-month myopia
will breath us opaque, displace the voices :

the vacuum will
cushion the edges, unclasp the coincidences :
                                    righten everything.

a go-around asks for no fuel:
        (shifts the reasons or paints them sky-dark).

"we are centripetal   ...profoundly self-same creatures,
...we are indivisible, insulated...
        prime numbers   not to be met with in nature..."

"...yes, we are strong and frail and rootless...
                                ...and our soil is
                                        sound in air..."
"yes, we are rootless...   ...the sky Antaeus...

                ... and should avoid these wind situations."

From the forms—solid, generic to the last vein
of their leaves'
reticulations;

from a rent in the hazardous and a deeper yet
cut
in the marrow of
ocular devolution
(eye-kneading, eye-replenishing, eye-fixation)
(eye-necessity, eye-submergence);

from other incisions,
unhealed,
in the random;

from our space confusion and cold,
cold other-space discordances;

from the target-circles—
dis-targeted;

from
the cycle of falls and vernal baptismal hands

we fall,—
we blossom in ice,
bloom the ice into splinters, scorch
the earth with our solar calluses,

ensemen it,
brew its grace,

reach out
for a half-hour
to hold back the hourglass' breath,
bind and pardon
our erroneous essences, blow through their lungs
our speech grains.—

We skin through the soil : its grey mouthfuls
word us,
speak through us—winnow
our names.

We stop our hearts
                    and listen:

            from ashes upwards,
            the earth begins
            our resurrection.

Doors what preserves
its shut   its open
what still
bangs with the drafts'
wheezing mode
of respiration

the
semi-autonomous bodies
open and shut   unaccountably
upon their nearing being
astral.

Porches what breaks
the bones of
the thresholds

melting the tallow
in premonition that all the soles
may enact a concurrence.

Windows   what
forms the habit of enduring

                    enduring

the runnels of water
　water
　　　　　　against the face.

　　eyes
　　funnel out and down
the palliating effect of this
　　　　vitreous mode
　　　　of being

　　uncurtained.

Paris (porte-à-faux)

arid alluvial
wrong city

boulevards crescendo at late midnight
swept hollow digest you out, you
only sleep out   sow your spirited spared
parts   miles away—your eye learns from sleep
to aim with them sharp—at the land of your coming.

Medusa
remedy

counter-lapidal
eyes, and flesh
disbelieving
    a posteriori.

                At night your memorial
                may disappear.

                You stand on the shore,

as quick as the sand.

City my needle, the only
vital part of the heart (rewritten body
spirits back into centuries), severs all predicates
and the beloved ones. Days do not add,
permeable to nothing but seasons. Fathers gone with the wind.

Mon ami, ne m'as tu pas aidée: *"…Ô ce sont des fantômes…"*

My heirloom, a single chair (rewritten body,
embroidered centuries, other vast rooms that restore me in
with a surgeon's precision)—a single chair.

The blessed string of eleven,—and St. Peter's dome
raises its forehead. Beyond this frontier I don't
carry my voice.

The cock never crows.

At quarter to 3 at Hanau harbour
blow out your lantern.
the solar trail stays the rest of the way
at your elbow. The annular rhythm of wheels
echoes
a farewell song
to Diogenes,
your life-long companion.

Walking in from the outskirts
of eternity, (a stopover at Nuremberg),—
along its unfenced ploughed furrows,
through fog and a grey
centripetal hour,
you stir sorrows with big ladles,

you drink your own
salt and pollen,
and shed or share the cloak.

For the past eyes
no wake to be seen

                        on the path you take
                        to the strait gate.

Sand flows from
the granted
into a single vessel:
a legitimate deduction
from the
Nowhere Almighty,—measurement by
essentiali-
sation.
One gathers the sand into
one's ever-pregnant
vocabulary.—

unless silence,
unless a painless
birth.

for Roman

We are shreds forgiven
blessed set at naught

via the side lane of a thousand years
a vicarious pardon comes
takes a seat
on the side
orchestrates our blood currents our
invisible intersections

invites us to happen
(the rhythm of tango and other
selected forms of the sleepless)

our private mornings
follow us closely,
we listen inside
to the dot-and-dash messages
sent through the septum.

At night
we coincide, and
rewind the clock winter-wise

and build a city
upon this city
from our raw material.

Notes

St. Anselm's art (p. 17):

> According to a medieval legend, Saint Anselm (not to be confused with St. Anselm of Canterbury) had a gift of healing wounds without a direct contact, simply by placing his hand on the bandage.

"It is time to start being towards winter, to sift apart..." (p. 20): for the last line of this poem cf. Mt. 8:22

Later in Vienna (p. 26):

> *Griensteidl* is the name of a café in Vienna, in former times a meeting place of Viennese literary circles. Today, having undergone a complete renovation, it is alas nothing more than a sterile tourist site.
>
> The line "*strongly beyond renovation as that angel...*" alludes to a poem by Paul Celan, 'Writing on the wall' (*"...a renovated angel ceases to be"*).
> The last lines of this poem are likewise an echo of another Celan poem 'Corona'.

"demagnetized hand still points..." (p. 39):

> *Cardinal Albergati* refers to the portrait of this person, by Jan van Eyck, now in the Kunsthistorisches Museum in Vienna.

'A limpid tear-pivoted essence...' (p. 40):

> the line "the impossible birds in the heaven" alludes to a note in Kafka's diary: "The crows maintain that a single crow could destroy the heavens. There is no doubt of that, but it proves nothing against the heavens, for heaven means, precisely, the impossibility of crows."

"come here / vicinity's miles distance..." (p. 43):

> Filippo Brunelleschi, an Italian Renaissance architect who formulated the principle of central perspective.

"ANOTHER DEGREE OF COMPLETION..." (P.51):
In the context of this poem, one should recall that unicorns are said not to procreate.

"FROST WILL PERFECT US..." (P.65):
Anthaeus, in Greek mythology, a half-giant who drew his strength from permanent contact with the earth (*Gaia,* the goddess of Earth, being his mother). He was thus defeated by Hercules who lifted him and held him above the ground until he lost his strength.

PARIS (PORTE-À-FAUX) (P.70):
porte-à-faux (French), a construction whereof one or several elements are supported by a part which, in itself, is supported by nothing and is suspended over the void.

"CITY MY NEEDLE..." (P.72):
a *needle* as a symbol has, here, the connotation of something vital and secret. The reference goes back to folklore, to an immortal being whose life and its source was hidden in a needle, which needle was hidden in an egg, egg in a goose, goose in a iron chest, etc. Only by breaking the tip of this needle could his life be taken.

perhaps a superfluous note: the "cock" of the last line points back to St. Peter.

"AT QUARTER TO 3 AT HANAU HARBOUR..." (P.73):
another superfluous note: allusion to the story of Diogenes wandering the streets of the city in full daylight, with his lantern lit, looking for a man.

"WALKING IN FROM THE OUTSKIRTS..." (P.74):
"...*share the cloak...*" refers to St. Martin; for the last line cf. Mt. 7:13.

"WE ARE SHREDS FORGIVEN..." (P.76):
septum (anatomy), a wall separating the chambers of the heart.